FIESTA

written by
Ellen Javernick

KAEDEN ❤ BOOKS™

Title: Fiesta
Copyright © 2013 Kaeden Corporation
Author: Ellen Javernick
Design: Signature Design

ISBN: 978-1-61181-433-0

PHOTOGRAPHY CREDITS pages 5, 6, 7 Lawrence Migdale; Daniel Aguilar;
Reuters Photo Archive

Published by:
    Kaeden Corporation
    P. O. Box 16190
    Rocky River, Ohio 44116
    1-(800)-890-READ(7323)
    www.kaeden.com

Printed in Guangzhou, China
NOR/0913/CA21301680

First edition 2004
Second edition 2013

Table of Contents

FIESTA

Hooray! There is a **fiesta** today.

Mexico has several differen kinds of fiestas celebrated for religious, national and local reasons.

We hear music.

Mariachi Band

violin

trumpet

guitar

guitarron

DANCING

We see dancers.
We dance too.

FLOWERS

We smell flowers.

FOOD

We eat and eat and eat.

Some traditional Mexican foods are tacos, quesadillas, tortillas, enchiladas, salsa and guacamole.

PIÑATA

We hit the piñata.
We run to get the candy.

piñata

stick

blindfold

FUN

The fiesta is fun.

Glossary

fiesta - a Spanish word that means party or festival

piñata - a papier-mâché figure filled with candy or toys that is suspended in the air so that blindfolded children may break it or knock it down with sticks to release the contents

Index